ParaSyte

7

HITOSHI IWAKI

TRANSLATED AND ADAPTED BY ANDREW CUNNINGHAM
LETTERED BY FOLTZ DESIGN

DEL
REY

BALLANTINE BOOKS · NEW YORK

A Del Rey Manga/Kodansha Trade Paperback Origina

Parasyte volume 7 copyright © 2003 by Hitoshi Iwaak
English translation copyright © 2009 by Hitoshi Iwaak

Published in the United States by Del Rey
an imprint of The Random House Publishing Group
a division of Random House, Inc., New York

DEL REY is a registered trademark and the Del Re
colophon is a trademark of Random House, Inc

Publication rights arranged through Kodansha Ltd

First published in Japan in 2003 by Kodansha
Ltd., Tokyo

ISBN 978-0-345-50035-9

Printed in the United States of America

www.delreymanga.com

1 2 3 4 5 6 7 8 9

Translator/adapter: Andrew Cunningham
Lettering: Foltz Design

CONTENTS

CHAPTER 50: WEAPON

WH-WHO IS THIS GUY?

IS HE A PARASITE? NO! DEFINITELY NOT!

STILL...

HE'S HUMAN! I DON'T KNOW HOW I KNOW THAT, BUT I DO.

SLEEPING.

MIGI...

THIS IS THE REAL MAN.

WHAT'S GOING ON? HE'S COMPLETELY DIFFERENT...

SHIVER

......

ARE YOU
HUMAN?

IS HE
HUMAN?

NAH...

I DON'T
THINK I'M
SPECIAL AT
ALL.

I GOT NO SPECIAL POWERS.

HMM... BASICALLY...

HOW CAN I TELL THE DIFFERENCE BETWEEN MONSTERS AND HUMANS?

...I'VE PLAYED ALL KINDS OF GAMES.

WITH HUMANS...

11

SO I KNOW A LOT ABOUT BASIC HUMAN NATURE.

THESE TOYS JUST BREAK SO EASILY...

ALL
THOSE
GAMES...
HEH HEH
HEH HEH
HEH HEH...

THEY KNOW
IF YOU'RE
ONE OF
THEM, OR
NOT...

STILL...MOST
ANIMALS
GOT THIS
INSTINCT,
RIGHT?

15

HELL, THERE WAS ANOTHER SPECIES WEARING CLOTHES AND WALKING THROUGH A CROWD.

THE FIRST TIME I FOUND ONE, SURE, I WAS SURPRISED...

I DID A LITTLE CROWD WATCHING... YOU MIGHT GET TWO OF THEM AN HOUR IF YOU WERE LUCKY.

I WAS ALWAYS A LITTLE WORRIED SOMEONE WOULD NOTICE *ME* WHEN I WAS OUT IN PUBLIC, SO EVERY TIME I SAW ONE OF THESE THINGS I WONDERED...WHY DID NOBODY ELSE NOTICE THEM? WHO WERE THEY, AND HOW COULD THEY WALK AROUND LOOKING LIKE THEY BELONGED HERE?

JUST MY ANIMAL INSTINCT, RIGHT? KEH HEH HEH HEH.

I KEPT MY DISTANCE. KNEW IT WAS A RISK.

I HAD HIGH HOPES FOR THEM, BUT..

WHAT COULD THIS UNKNOWN SPECIES BE UP TO?

17

IT WAS NOTHING. SAME CRAP I ALWAYS DID.

URP...

Y-YOU SON OF A BITCH!

GOTTA CLEAN UP WHEN YOU FINISH PLAYING...

SCATTERED EVERY-WHERE...

CRAP!

DON'T MOVE!

I DIDN'T DO IT THIS TIME!

IT WASN'T ME!!

N-NO!!

AWW...

THIS TIME!?

I THINK WE CAUGHT A BIG ONE HERE!

BLAARGGHH!

YOU GOTTA BE KID-DING!

I'VE SEEN YOUR FACE! YOU'RE ON THE WANTED POSTER!

HOW LONG ARE THEY...?

・・・・・・・・

SHOULD WE...?

HIRAMA-SAN...

URAGAMI....

BUT NOW HE'S SCARED.

IZUMI SHINICHI DIDN'T FLINCH AT ALL WHILE WE INTER- ROGATED HIM...

NOPE.

HE MIGHT HAVE POTENTIAL, BUT YOU'D HAVE TO TRAIN HIM.

HUNH...

WHAT DO YOU MEAN, URAGAMI?

WHAT?

JUST MY MIND PLAYING TRICKS ON ME, BUT FOR A SECOND I THOUGHT I SAW SOMETHING NOT QUITE HUMAN IN THE DEPTHS OF HIS EYES.

CONFUSED HOW?

SOMETHING ELSE HAS BEEN BUGGING ME. I'M CONFUSED.

I LOOKED CAREFULLY, BUT THERE WAS NO SIGN OF IT.

DUDE, DON'T SHOUT IN MY EAR. IT WAS NOTHING.

WHAT!?

OH. WELL, THANK YOU...

......

I THINK THAT GUY'S REALLY SCARY LOOKING.

IZUMI-KUN, WHAT DO YOU THINK.

WHEW...

WE'LL HAVE YOU STAY AT A HOTEL FOR THE NEXT FEW DAYS.

OH, I'M SURE WE WON'T NEED...

WE'LL SEND GUARDS.

WHEN YOU VISIT YOUR HOME, BE SURE TO CALL US.

I INSIST.

NO.

THE ONE TAMURA REIKO HANDED TO YOU?

ABOUT THE BABY...

UH, HIRAMA-SAN...

BUT WHEN YOU'RE SURE IT'S AN ORDINARY BABY...

AFTER ALL, IT WAS RAISED BY A MONSTER...

WE'RE STILL CHECKING IT.

UM...ER...

WHY DO YOU ASK?

IN THAT CASE, IT WILL BE TURNED OVER TO THE PROPER AGENCIES.

EH...

IF YOU CLAIM TO BE A RELATIVE OF TAMURA REIKO, WE COULD LEAVE IT WITH YOU...

SHINICHI?

AH....HA HA...

I'M KIDDING.

SO, WHAT SHALL WE EAT TONIGHT?

ITY HOTEL GRE

THE DEPTHS OF HIS EYES? HOW COULD I TELL?

MM...OKAY, I GUESS...

I WAS GETTING PRETTY SICK OF THE LAB'S A LUNCH...

HOW WAS THE B LUNCH?

REALLY?

WANT A BATH?

AFTER YOU...

OKAY.

WHEWWWWW....

THUNK

26

WHO WAS THAT? SCARES ME JUST REMEMBERING HIM... I'VE SEEN ALL KINDS OF MAN-EATING MONSTERS, BUT...

SHINICHI.

YEAH...WHILE YOU WERE ASLEEP I MET THIS REALLY SCARY GUY...

PHYSICALLY AND MENTALLY.

IT SEEMS LIKE YOU'RE EXHAUSTED...

HEY, MIGI.

...HE WAS A KILLER.

YEAH, BUT I'M SURE...

HUMAN?

27

I JUST DON'T UNDERSTAND ANY MORE.

AND I JUST...

...SAVED ME.

...BUT A MAN-EATING MONSTER LIKE TAMURA REIKO...

THERE ARE HUMANS AS UNBELIEV-ABLY SCARY AS THAT GUY...

...WHAT SHE DID.

I STILL CAN'T COMPRE-HEND...

...IN MY CHEST...

THE HOLE...

PARASITES AND HUMANS ARE PART OF THE SAME FAMILY.

....

YEAH... I UNDER- STAND.

BUT THAT HIRAMA MAN SEEMS TO HAVE A JOB FOR YOU...

...MAKE SURE YOU SHOW NOTHING.

SHINICHI, I FELL ASLEEP HALF- WAY THROUGH, SO I DON'T KNOW EVERY- THING THAT HAPPENED.

I MEAN, YOU...

REALLY?

WHAT?

DAD'S COMING OUT.

SWISH

vvv...

BROO

BROO

HOTEL GR

......

SEND HIM IN.

LIEUTENANT COLONEL YAMAGISHI TO SEE YOU.

WHAT?

NICE TO MEET YOU, INSPECTOR HIRAMA.

BEFORE WE MEET WITH OUR SUPERIORS, I THOUGHT WE SHOULD ALL BE ON THE SAME PAGE.

AND NOW THERE ARE RUMORS YOU'RE HEADED FOR SUPERINTENDENT?

BUT YOU WERE ONLY AN INSPECTOR BEFORE ALL THIS.

YOU JEST.

LIEUTENANT.

WHILE L.C. YAMAGISHI TOOK THE INSIDE— IDENTIFYING THE ENEMY, AND FIGHTING THEM.

SO HIRAMA-KUN APPROACHED THINGS FROM THE OUTSIDE...

MM?

BEFORE THAT, DIRECTOR...

BUT THERE IS NOT MUCH POINT IN OUR KEEPING HIM. I BELIEVE HE SHOULD BE TURNED OVER TO THE INNER CIRCLE AND INCORPO- RATED INTO THEIR STRATEGIES.

THIS MAN URAGAMI— I MENTIONED HIM THE OTHER DAY—HE COULD PROVE EXTREMELY USEFUL.

32

THAT WOULD CAUSE TOO MANY PROBLEMS. A MAN LIKE HIM IN THE MIDDLE OF A HIGHLY TRAINED UNIT WILL DERAIL THINGS AT A CRITICAL JUNCTURE.

BUT THIS PSYCHIC IS A KILLER, RIGHT?

I'M GRATEFUL FOR YOUR OFFER, HIRAMA.

BUT NOW THAT WE'VE MADE TWO MOVING SCANNERS, I DOUBT WE NEED THEM.

EYES? HMM...

I'M NOT SUGGESTING HE BE PART OF A UNIT. HE WILL SIMPLY BE AN EXTRA PAIR OF EYES.

SORRY, BUT I SIMPLY CAN'T ACCEPT THAT...VERY POLICEMAN-LIKE OPINION. YOU KEEP THINKING OF THEM AS HUMAN.

OUR ENEMY WILL NOT MOVE LIKE SHEEP WHEN CHASED BY DOGS.

....

WHAT WE ARE DOING IS NOT DETECTIVE WORK; IT IS PEST CONTROL.

YOU MAY HAVE DIFFERENT APPROACHES AND DIVISIONS, BUT WE CAN'T AFFORD CONFLICT BETWEEN THEM...

I'M GLAD I SUMMONED YOU HERE FIRST.

AFTER ALL, THE TOFUKUYAMA-SHI TOWN HALL IS IN THE CENTER OF TOWN.

CHAPTER 50: THE END

34

CHAPTER 51: BEARING

38

......

CERTAINLY, JUST A MOMENT...

CAN WE PUSH IT BACK A BIT?

NAKAI-KUN, THE 3:00 MEETING...

CLK

......

WHERE ARE YOU GOING, MR. MAYOR?

BEEP BEEP BEEP

40

SECRETARY (?)

SECRETARY (HUMAN)

41

IS SHE ALIVE?

TAMURA REIKO?

IT'S NOT A STRONG POSSIBILITY...

ONE OF THE THREE MANGLED CORPSES THEY FOUND AT THE CONSTRUCTION SITE WAS A WOMAN...

THERE'S NO OTHER REASON FOR HER AND HER CHILD TO FALL OUT OF CONTACT.

...WAS KUSANO?

ONE OF THOSE THREE...

BUT...

SUCH A SHAME WE LET THE OTHER SIDE COLLECT ALL THE FRAGMENTS.

: : : : :

AN ANTI-PARASITE SQUAD.

THEY APPEAR TO BE A SPECIAL TASK FORCE.

BUT NO HUMAN WOULD BE ABLE TO TAKE OUT THREE OF US AT THE SAME TIME.

IF WE HAD THE BODIES, WE'D KNOW WHO KILLED THEM.

YOU MEAN TAMURA REIKO...?

GOTO-SAN.

AND I BELIEVE IT'S BEYOND THE CAPABILITIES OF THAT BOY AND HIS HAND.

WE'RE AT A VERY SIGNIFICANT DISADVANTAGE.

I DON'T KNOW. BUT IT'S CLEAR THAT SOMETHING CAPABLE OF FIGHTING US IS LURKING VERY CLOSE AT HAND.

EASIER SAID THAN DONE.

I SAY WE MOVE THE COLONY.

CERTAINLY, TAMURA-SAN HAD A VERY UNIQUE WAY OF THINKING. BUT IT'S HARD TO BELIEVE SHE WOULD TURN AGAINST US.

BUT IF THE ENEMY HAS KILLED HER...

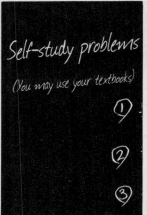

Self-study problems

(You may use your textbooks)

① ② ③

DO YOU UNDERSTAND THIS? YOU'VE MISSED SO MUCH SCHOOL...

IZUMI-KUN....
IZUMI-KUN...

· · · · · · · ·

OR WERE YOU KEEPING UP AT HOME?

MMM...

WAIT, YOU'RE AHEAD OF ALL OF US NOW?

OKAY, TURN THEM IN.

SURE.

MAKE A COPY, GIVE THEM BACK.

I'M COMPLETELY LOST!

BORROW MY NOTES?

PLEASE.

ONLY 1000 YEN.

RIIIIGHT...

HE'S GOT A GIRL-FRIEND.

OH, COME ON.

OBVIOUS MUCH, AKEMI?

BANG

COME ON!

17.5

HAHH
HAHH
HAHH
HAHH

TKK

TKK

TKK

TKK

RUN LIKE YOU MEAN IT, OR YOU'LL REGRET IT YOUR WHOLE LIFE!

THIS MAY WELL BE THE LAST TIME YOU EVER RUN THE ONE HUNDRED METER!

THIS IS YOUR LAST CHANCE TO GET YOUR TIME RECORDED!

LISTEN UP!

EVERYTHING THAT GUY SAYS IS OVERBLOWN...

GET REAL.

WAIT! WAIT! HOLD IT RIGHT THERE!

I'VE BEEN MEANING TO SAY THIS...

YOU, THERE! IZUMI!

NO NEED TO SHOUT...

AT THIS RATE YOU'LL NEVER MAKE ANYTHING OF YOURSELF!

I'VE NEVER ONCE SEEN YOU EVEN TRY!

YOUR SCORES ARE ALL OVER THE PLACE!

HEH HEH HEH...

BE A MAN AND GIVE EVERYTHING YOU GOT!

I CAN'T DO THAT...

TRY FOR ONCE!

SOMEONE MAKE HIM SHUT UP.

THE LAST
TIME?

BANG

SO MUCH FOR
HIGH SCHOOL...

WHEW...

T-TEN POINT FIVE!?

WOW...

GOOD THING I DIDN'T GO FOR NINE...

IF YOU WERE THAT FAST...!!

IZUMI! YOU... WHY NOW!?

58

THAT WAS AMAZING, IZUMI!

A NEW SCHOOL RECORD.

NOT EVEN ON THE TRACK TEAM...

DON'T PLAY DUMB!

WHAT WAS?

HA HA HA HA HA

WAS IT?

WAS IT?

EH?

WHY IS IT YOU ALWAYS CHANGE IN THE CORNER LIKE THAT?

I'VE BEEN WONDERING FOR A WHILE...

59

I'M JUST NOT THAT STRONG...

UM, NO...

SO IS YOUR BODY A SECRET?

AND I'VE NEVER SEEN YOU SWIM...

AH!

WE'RE ALL DUDES HERE!

COME ON!

E-EXCUSE ME.

NAH...

WELL...

OH, UM...

SMACK

TWIT.

ONLY SIX MORE MONTHS...

YEAH...

WHAT?

YOU OKAY?

I CAN GRADUATE.

GRADUATE!?

YOU MISSED A LOT OF DAYS...

OH, I'M FINE.

: : : : : :

I LIKED HIGH SCHOOL, MOSTLY.

...HAPPENED.

SO MUCH....

YEAH.

BUT THERE WERE GOOD THINGS, TOO.

WHAT ABOUT THEM?

WHAT ABOUT ENTRANCE EXAMS?

OH, RIGHT, IZUMI-KUN...

I GOTTA STUDY...

WHEN I
GET TO
COLLEGE...

MM?

COME.

WE WILL WIN!!

!

AND I DON'T KNOW WHAT IT IS.

BUT THERE IS ONE THING WE LACK.

WE ARE 99 PERCENT READY!

YOU MIGHT.

HE'S NOT THE ONLY ONE HERE TRYING VERY HARD TO FORGET...

WHY IS IT ALWAYS IZUMI-KUN?

BUT TURN THE CORNER...

A NORMAL SCHOOL ROAD.

THIS IS SUPPOSED TO BE AN ORDINARY ROAD...

AND IT'S COVERED IN BLOOD!

CHAPTER 51: THE END

CHAPTER 52: SURROUNDED

THE DAY ARRIVED...

ブォ——— VROOM...

SCREECH

TKK TKK Do

キキ
SCREECH.

MM? NO, NOT AT ALL.

SORRY, BUT WE'VE GOT A WHOLE BUNCH OF SCHOOLBUSES ARRIVING HERE TODAY. DO YOU MIND PARKING OVER THERE?

WE NEED THIS PLACE...

IT LIES BETWEEN THE ENTRANCE AND THE WEST GATE, THERE'S PLENTY OF ROOM, AND THE SOUTHEAST CORNER IS ALMOST IMPOSSIBLE TO SEE FROM THE MAIN BUILDING.

THE SECOND PARKING LOT HERE MAKES THE IDEAL HUNTING GROUND.

BUT WE CAN'T JUST SEND IN TANKS.

BUSES...!

WE'RE USING BUSES.

‥‥‥‥

LARGE BUSES, LIKE THEY USE FOR SCHOOL FIELD TRIPS, WITH THE CURTAINS DRAWN.

WE'LL LINE UP EIGHT OF THEM LIKE THIS...

VROOM

AS SOON AS THE BUSES ARE IN POSITION, THE OUTER CIRCLE—THE POLICE—WILL SURROUND CITY HALL.

MOST OF THE BUILDING IS SURROUNDED BY HEDGES...WHICH ARE MORE LIKE FLOWER BEDS. THEY ARE NOT VERY TALL, SO WE WILL BE COMPLETELY VISIBLE FROM INSIDE.

LOOKS LIKE THE RIOT POLICE...

A MILITARY COUP?

EH? WHAT!?

SERIOUSLY?

WHAT ARE THEY THINKING?

THERE ARE FAR MORE HUMANS IN THE BUILDING!

NICE WORK BY THE POLICE...

ZAA ザ"
ZAA ザ"
ZAA ザ"

AND WHILE EVERYONE INSIDE IS LOOKING OUT THE WINDOWS...

ROGER!

START THE BROAD-CAST.

WHAM!

MOVE TO THE CORNER OF THE ROOM! WE MEAN YOU NO HARM!

EEEK!

YIKES!

T-TO WHAT?

WE'RE ALL GONNA LISTEN TOGETHER.

LISTEN CAREFULLY! THIS IS EXTREMELY URGENT!

EMERGENCY! EMERGENCY! ALL PERSONNEL!

MY NAME IS MIZUSHIMA, FROM THE TOFUKUYAMA POLICE.

THIS IS EXTREMELY URGENT! PLEASE LISTEN CAREFULLY!

GRIN

BUT WHY ARE THEY POINTING GUNS AT US?

WHEW...

OH, GOOD...

BEGIN OPERATION GUIDE SQUAD! SEAL ALL ENTRANCES TO THE MAIN BUILDING AND THE ASSEMBLY BUILDING, SPLIT UP ALONG THE THREE STAIRCASES AND GATHER IN THE MAIN HALL.

EXACTLY, IDENTIFY YOURSELF AS POLICE... JAPANESE PEOPLE PANIC WHEN THE ARMY HAS THE MICROPHONE...

CURRENTLY HE IS HIDING OUT NEAR THE ROOM.

HE IS OF AVERAGE SIZE AND WEIGHT, WEARING A YELLOW T-SHIRT AND JEANS, AND IS BLEEDING FROM A WOUND IN HIS STOMACH.

A MAN WITH A GUN HAS ENTERED THE BUILDING.

DO NOT STEP OUTSIDE! IT IS VERY DANGEROUS.

I REPEAT, IT IS VERY DANGEROUS OUTSIDE!

OH...IS THAT ALL?

SEEMS LIKE AN AWFUL LOT OF THEM...

EVERYONE IN THE BUILDING, PLEASE MOVE TO THE MAIN HALL.

EVERYONE IN THE BUILDING SHOULD GATHER IN THE MAIN HALL ON THE FIRST FLOOR.

TKK TKK TKK TKK

FOLLOW ALL INSTRUCTIONS THE OFFICERS IN THE HALL GIVE YOU.

MR. MAYOR!!

MR. MAYOR!

MR. MAYOR! THIS IS TERRIBLE!

THIS IS CLEARLY NO JOKING MATTER.

CALM YOURSELF. WE MUST FOLLOW THEIR INSTRUCTIONS.

THESE HUMANS MEAN BUSINESS.

NOT ONE OF THEM HAS JURIS- DICTION HERE...

THESE ARE POLICE? HA!

88

THEY COULD CHECK THEM ONE BY ONE, BUT THE MOMENT THEY FIND A PARASITE... PANDEMONIUM.

BUT WITH ALL THESE INNOCENT HUMANS HERE...

THEY WOULDN'T JUST KILL ALL OF THEM... WOULD THEY?

AH! THE MAYOR!

FRONT ENTRANCE

BACK A LITTLE MORE...STOP!

ALL FURTHER ADJUST-MENTS ARE AUTOMATIC.

WING

ALL CITIZENS SHOULD STAY INSIDE! IF YOU ARE OUTSIDE, REMAIN OUT OF SIGHT OF CITY HALL!

THERE IS A MAN WITH A GUN ON THE ROOF OF CITY HALL!

MY!

HE IS ON THE NORTH SIDE OF THE ROOF.

WE'VE RECEIVED INFORMATION ABOUT THE CRIMINAL.

MM, MM.

THANK GOD!

WE ARE NOW GOING TO EVACUATE THE BUILDING THROUGH THE WEST GATE, IN HIS BLIND SPOT.

WE WILL BE MOVING YOU OUT IN GROUPS OF SEVEN.

BUT IF WE MOVE TOO MANY OF YOU AT ONCE HE MIGHT NOTICE.

THAT'S ALL?

EHH? ONLY SEVEN?

THESE MEN WILL RECEIVE CONSTANT RADIO UPDATES ON THE CRIMINAL'S BEHAVIOR!

DON'T WORRY! THERE WILL BE TWO GUARDS IN FRONT AND TWO GUARDS BEHIND!

MUTTER

MUTTER

BUT WHO FIRST?

HARDLY.

AFTER YOU, MR. MAYOR.

THEN THE WOMEN.

CHILDREN AND ELDERLY FIRST.

TCH...

CITY EMPLOYEES SHOULD BE LAST.

HOW SHOULD I KNOW?

DON'T KNOW WHAT I'M HERE FOR.

BUT THIS IS AWESOME, LIKE A WAR!

I CAN'T TELL A DAMN THING ON THIS MONITOR!

AH...

HEY! THAT KID!

SHUT UP!

FIRST THE ARMY, THEN A SERIAL KILLER, AND NOW A KID!?

HEE HEE HEE HEE! WHAT WAS THAT!?

....

ANY OF THEM THERE?

NOT A VERY HIGH QUALITY IMAGE, BUT YOU CAN SEE WHAT'S HAPPENING IN THE HALL.

I DON'T SEE ANY...

THIS STRANGE ONE, WITH SEVERAL PARASITES IN ONE BODY...

HMM...EITHER NOT THERE, OR WITH A DIFFERENT FACE?

STRANGE ONE...

NO GUARANTEE THAT HE ISN'T THE ONLY ONE.

ONE MORE THING. THIS CITY'S MAYOR, HIROKAWA...

SOUNDED LIKE HE WAS THE ONLY ONE OF HIS KIND.

ACCORDING TO TAMURA REIKO, THIS FIVE-IN-ONE WAS CALLED GOTO...

HE'S THE KEY TO ALL OF THIS... WHAT WAS SHE GOING TO TELL ME?

OKAY, FIRST GROUP OF SEVEN!

I FEEL SORRY FOR THE CRIMINAL...

SUCH A SCARY WEAPON.

THE FIRST SEVEN.

CLEAR.

ALL HUMAN.

THIS TIME... NO PARASITES.

NEXT GROUP!

YOU SURE THIS THING'S WORKING?

I'M SURE!

NOTHING.

NEXT GROUP...

MIGI, YOU KNOW HOW MANY THERE ARE?

LESS OF THEM THAN WE THOUGHT...

NOT FROM THAT SCREEN. WE'RE A LITTLE TOO FAR BUT... PRETTY MANY.

RIGHT, LET'S GO BY TENS.

FOUND ONE!

THERE!

LADIES FIRST.

CHAPTER 52: THE END

HE'S A WITNESS.

LOOKS LIKE A HIGH SCHOOL KID...

WHO IS THIS, HIRAMA-SAN?

A FEW DAYS EARLIER

WE SHOULD TAKE THIS INTO ACCOUNT.

HE'S SOME SORT OF PROTOTYPE? SOUNDS STRONG.

NOT JUST IN THE HEAD, BUT PARASITES IN THE HANDS AND FEET?

OH?

: : : : : : : :

DON'T WORRY ABOUT IT BEING AN AMATEUR'S OPINION, BUT CAN YOU THINK OF ANY WEAPONS THAT MIGHT BE MORE EFFECTIVE THAN A PISTOL AGAINST THIS PROTOTYPE PARASITE?

YOU WATCHED HIRAMA TAKE ONE OF THESE OUT THE OTHER DAY...

SO...

YEAH...

BWA HA HA HA HA! EXCUSE ME!

A FLAME-THROWER?

BUT WE'RE IN THE MIDDLE OF TOWN, AND WILL BE FIGHTING INDOORS. IF SOMEONE ON FIRE RUNS AROUND IT COULD BURN THE WHOLE PLACE DOWN AND RUIN OUR PLANS.

NOT BAD.

HMM....

DON'T WORRY! HE MAY HAVE SEVERAL PARASITES, BUT HE ONLY HAS ONE HEART.

WE CAN TAKE HIM. WITH THE WEAPONS WE ALREADY HAVE.

LADIES FIRST.

AND HER FIGHTING ABILITY IS FAR MORE THAN ANY MERE HUMAN...

A FACE LIKE THAT CAN TURN INSTANTLY INTO A BLADE?

WE CAN'T TREAT THEM LIKE ANIMALS, DAMAGE THEM, WEAKEN THEM...WE HAVE TO DEFEAT THEM INSTANTLY, BLASTING THEM AWAY.

WHAT WE NEED TO FEAR MOST IS THEIR COMPLETE LACK OF PAIN.

AND THE BEST WAY TO STOP A MACHINE IS TO DESTROY THE MOTOR.

THEY ARE NOT ALIVE. THEY ARE MACHINES CONTROLLED BY THE DEVIL.

IN OTHER WORDS, SHOTGUNS.

THAN DESTRUCTION.

WHAT WE NEED IS LESS PENETRATION...

WE WILL FILL EACH CARTRIDGE WITH 16.8MM SHOT, SLIGHTLY SMALLER THAN A PACHINKO BALL.

BUT THE HEART IS SEVERAL CENTIMETERS INSIDE THE BODY, AND THE NORMAL SIZED SHOT WOULD NEVER REACH THAT FAR.

RODGER.

MM?

SHH...

?

SLIP

OKAY, EVERYONE, THIS WAY.

IF WE AIM WELL, WITH ONE BLAST...

EH....?

TKK TKK "7

UNH...

PSHT

SWISH

CLUNK

AUGH!

WAIT FOR IT...

DON'T SHOOT...

YIKES!

WE DID IT!

ONE SHOT-GUN BLAST...

ONE SHOT!

GOT IT!

RIGHT, CHANGE THE PASSAGE! CLEAN UP THE BODY!

THAT'S WHAT THEY CALL THE EGG OF COLUMBUS.

SO SIMPLE... ONE BLAST WITH A LARGE-SHOT CARTRIDGE...

VRROOM

WHAT WAS THAT?

MURMUR

GUN-SHOTS!?

PLEASE REMAIN QUIET!

EVERY-ONE!

WE BELIEVE IT TO HAVE BEEN A WARNING SHOT, BUT WE'RE GOING TO WAIT A FEW MINUTES BEFORE CONTINUING THE EVACUATION.

THE MAN ON THE ROOF APPEARS TO HAVE FIRED HIS WEAPON HARMLESSLY FROM THE OTHER SIDE OF THE BUILDING.

MM, MM...

GOOD PLAN, FOR HUMANS.

SHE DIED... INSTANTLY.

: : :

SO...NOW WHAT?

RIGHT, COME ON!

EVACU-ATION RESUMES

HERE EITHER.

NONE HERE.

NOTHING AGAIN.

NO.

WERE THERE ONLY A FEW OF THEM?

ARE THEY ONTO US?

WHY DON'T THEY SEND ANOTHER?

WHAT IS IT, INSPECTOR HIRAMA?

WHAT?

CONNECT ME TO LC YAMAGISHI.

ALL THAT PLANNING AND WE ONLY GOT ONE.

YEAH, I READ THOSE, TOO. THE MONSTER TELEPATHY?

THAT UNCONFIRMED INFORMATION IN THE NOTES THAT PRIVATE DETECTIVE LEFT... EXPLAINS THIS, DOESN'T IT?

WE SHOULD BE CAUTIOUS! I'LL SEND URAGAMI IN TO HELP.

BUT IF THAT'S THE CASE, FINE. GATHER THEM ALL TOGETHER.

WHAT IS IT?

THE MAYOR...

HOLD ON A SECOND.

BUT THAT MAN...

THERE'S A MATTER WE MUST DISCUSS TODAY IN ONE OF THE MEETING ROOMS. LET US THROUGH.

THERE'S ONLY ONE OF THEM, AND HE'S ON THE ROOF! JUST TURN OFF THE ELEVATORS AND BLOCK THE STAIRS.

WE'LL DO THE PLANNING!

THE MEETING ROOM IS JUST UPSTAIRS. DON'T WORRY.

BUT...AT A TIME LIKE THIS...

FORTY? DON'T LET THEM ESCAPE. HURRY AND CHECK THE OTHER EVACUEES.

AT LEAST FORTY.

HOW MANY ARE WITH HIM?

RIGHT AWAY.

OKAY, SEND IN YOUR PSYCHIC KILLER.

INSPECTOR HIRAMA!

・・・・・・

TAKE THE HANDCUFFS OFF AT LEAST! WHAT IF SOMETHING HAPPENS?

FINE.

I MEAN, I'M SURROUNDED BY COPS!

I'M NOT GONNA RUN!

NO.

· · · · · · · ·

· · · · · · · ·

WE'VE GOT TO DO MORE! WE CAN IDENTIFY THEM, TOO!

MIGI! HEY, MIGI!

PLEASE COOPERATE!!

WE CAN'T!!

IF WE'RE GOING TO DO SOMETHING, IT'LL HAVE TO BE WHILE THERE'S STILL A CROWD OF HUMANS...

HOW DARE YOU AIM GUNS AT CITIZENS!!

WHAT?

EH?

EH? OH...

AREN'T WE GOING? I'D LIKE TO EVACUATE...

CHAPTER 53: THE END

CHAPTER 54: PACIFICATION

MM? YOU SAY SOMETHING?

EITHER WAY, I'M...

OFFICER... OFFICER!

TROMP

TROMP

NOPE.

TROMP

TROMP

TROMP

MM? HEY, WAIT! I CAN'T TELL LIKE THIS!

OH, THIS CAR.

WAIT, STOP!

AH!

SINGLE-FILE LINE, PLEASE!

WHAT!? AAAUGH! AAAHH!

! TROMP TROMP

IN THE LINE! THREE OF THEM!

STOP!! W-WAIT!

CAN'T LET THEM GET AWAY!

AH!

TKK TKK TKK

GAH!

BAM!

WHAT!?

THAT WAS A HUMAN.

AH...

EH?

MOVE BACK.

H-HOW HORRIBLE...

SPLAT

MOVE THREE STEPS BACKWARDS SO WE CAN CHECK.

URAGAMI! COME ON, URAGAMI!

OH, HE IS SO DEAD.

UM....?

KILL HIM!!

SHOOT HIM NOW!

HOW ABOUT HIM?

134

AIEEEE!

SMASH!

GRUGH...

A MON- STER!!

NOOOOOO!

AAAHHHH!

AHHH!

THUMP

EH?

グッ GRAB

WH-WHAT THE
HELL ARE YOU
DOING?

UNH...

EEK!

WOAH...

WHAT ARE YOU DOING!?

HIM!

AUGH!

PSHH...

BAM!

RIGHT!

NO! DON'T SHOOT!

DO NOT STAND UP! EVERYONE WHO STANDS UP WILL BE SHOT!

HOW CAN YOU...

HOLD ON!

BAM

HMPH. HUMAN?

COUGH...

AH...

IF YOU ARE HUMAN, THEN DO AS WE SAY! YOU'LL BE HOME IN NO TIME!

DON'T YOU GET IT!? THERE ARE PARASITES AMONG YOU!!

CAPTAIN!

OVER HERE, KILLER!

WE WILL CLEAN THE REST OF THE BUILDING.

YES, SIR!

YOU'RE IN CHARGE HERE.

YOU'RE THE BEST WAY WE HAVE OF IDENTIFYING THEM. THANKS.

ACK!

RIGHT?

THAT'S THE POT CALLING THE KETTLE BLACK...

WHAT!? I CAN'T HEAR YOU!

MUMBLE

DRASTIC TIMES CALL FOR...

OKAY, FIRST ROW, STAND UP SLOWLY!

HANDS BEHIND YOUR HEAD!

TWITCH

GRAB ガッ

・・・・・

SPLAT

GUH...

BAM

BAMM!

GAH!

SLICE!

EEEK!

PLOP

KA-CHUNK

EEEEEEEK!

EEEEEEEE!

URP!

BAM!

I TOLD YOU NOT TO STAND UP!!

YOU... !!

SPLAT

. . . . . .

BAM

BAM

TAP

TAP

TAP

SO COULD YOU.

YOU COULD GET THROUGH THE BARRIER EASILY.

WHY NOT TRY TO ESCAPE?

I WANT TO WATCH HOW THEY FIGHT A LITTLE LONGER... WHAT ABOUT YOU?

I DON'T SEE MUCH POINT IN RUNNING.

DO AS YOU LIKE.

OH?

YOU MEN TAKE THE MEETING HALL, THE REST OF US WILL COVER THE MAIN BUILDING.

BUT HOW WILL YOU TELL...?

SEND THE KILLER TO THE MEETING HALL F.

YOU'RE A KILLER, TOO...

URAGAMI.

・・・・・・

!?

I'M STARTING TO GET THE HANG OF THIS.

DON'T WORRY.

BANG

EEEEK!
ぎゃあああ
きゃーっあっ

SIGH... THIS BLOWS.

DON'T PUSH ME!

URAGAMI!! THIS WAY, QUICKLY!

BOTH OF THEM.

THIS IS STUPID... THEY'RE HUMAN.

AHHHH-HHHH!

BUT IF I WEREN'T HERE, THEY'D BE FULL OF HOLES.

SUCH PEACE.

WHAT WERE YOU THINKING!? AT A TIME LIKE THIS!?

MM?

BUT HOW DID YOU KNOW?

GUH... GRAH...

SEE?

IF YOU SEE SOME-BODY, SHOOT THEM.

HUNH?

HE WASN'T IN THE MAIN HALL.

THE HUMANS WERE IN CONTROL FROM THE BEGIN-NING.

MAKING THAT OBVIOUS KEPT THE PANIC TO A MINIMUM.

THE SOLDIERS' PURPOSE WAS NEVER THE PROTECTION OF THE CITIZENS, BUT THE DESTRUCTION OF THE ENEMY.

SEVERAL HUMANS DIED, BUT ALL THE PARASITES WERE EXTERMINATED.

ド"、ノ、 BAM!

ｱｱｱｱｱ..
RATATATATA...

SO...

WE ARE VERY WEAK. CLUSTERS OF CELLS UNABLE TO SURVIVE ON THEIR OWN.

HEH HEH HEH HEH...

CHAPTER 54: THE END

SO TRY TO BE NICE.

BAM

BAM!

YOU'RE OUR 'EYES.'

DO I HAVE TO BE IN FRONT?

AH!

WHOOSH

W-WAIT, PLEASE! I'M NOT ONE OF THEM!

STOP!

P-PLEASE!

AUUGH!

SHOOT!

BAM!

EEK!

SHOOT HIM NOW!

LEARN TO AIM.

. . . .

SPLAT

AFTER HIM!

TKK

夕

夕ッ

TKK

BAM

BAM

. . . .

UNH....
GUH...

DESTROYING
THE BODY
WITH LARGE
SHOT...

VERY
EFFECTIVE.

HE LOOKS LIKE ONE, BUT JUST IN CASE...

WHAT ABOUT HIM?

!

JUST SHOOT ALL OF THEM...

THIS BLOWS...

OKAY, OKAY...

AAUUUG-GGHHHH!!

．．．．．
？

URAGAMI!?
COME
BACK!

AIIEEEE!

MORE
SPACE
OVER
HERE.

COME.

．．．．．．．

WHAT?

I WANTED TAKE ON THE LOT OF YOU.

STOP! URAGAMI!

HAHH HAHH HAHH HAHH.

DIDN'T YOU *SEE* HIM?

EHHH?

HAHH HAHH HAHH...

DAMN YOU! WE'RE NOT LETTING YOU GET AWAY!

HEH...

WHAT!?

EH? HE LOOKED... HUMAN TO YOU?

BLAM

BLAM

BLAM

BLAM

FIRE!!

WHAT'S THAT SOUND?

FROM INSIDE HIS BODY!

AIIIEEEE!!

HMM... YOU GAVE ME SO *MANY*...

SPLAT

ACK...

PTT

NO WAY... SHOT PELLETS!?

TINK TINK

TINK TINK

HIS ARMS!

AUUUG-GGHHH!

UNH...

GUHAAA

SMASH

SMASH

SMASH

THUNK

THUNK

THUNK

THUNK

UNH...

KAFF...

OH, BODY ARMOR.

SO MANY SURVIVED?

RRAGH!

BAM

178

DO I GET TO MOCK YOU NOW?

KAFF

IT'LL TAKE ANOTHER THIRTY SECONDS TO FINISH YOU OFF.

DO AS I SAY!

LIKE HELL!

WE'RE GOING BACK, URAGAMI!

ASSEMBLY HALL

GREETINGS, GENTLEMEN.

DON'T JUST STAND THERE, TAKE A SEAT.

BUT THE TOOLS YOU ARE HOLDING IN YOUR HANDS SHOULD BE USED FOR SOMETHING, SOMETHING FAR MORE IMPORTANT.

YOU WIN TODAY. NO SPECIES IS BETTER AT KILLING THAN HUMANS.

WHAT'S HE TALKING ABOUT?

PRESERVING THE BALANCE OF THE BIOSPHERE.

YOUR TRUE PURPOSE.

PRUNING.

IN THE NEAR FUTURE, YOU WILL ALL REALIZE...

...HOW VITAL IT IS TO REDUCE THE HUMAN POPULATION.

COVER THE SIDES!

AND A FEW YEARS LATER YOU WILL REALIZE HOW CRITICAL OUR EXISTENCE IS, AND SEEK TO PRESERVE OUR SPECIES.

YOU WILL REALIZE THAT A NATURAL ENEMY IS A NECESSARY EVIL.

SHORTLY AFTER THAT, POLLUTING WILL BECOME MORE SERIOUS A CRIME THAN MURDER.

AT LAST, THE BALANCE WILL BE RESTORED!

THAT NATURAL ENEMY CAPS THE BEAUTIFUL PYRAMID OF NATURE, JUST ABOVE HUMANITY!

ON EARTH SOMEONE THOUGHT...

WE HAVE TO PROTECT THE FUTURE OF *ALL* LIFE...

ENVIRONMENTAL PRESERVATION AND ANIMAL PROTECTION ARE ALL DISTORTED EFFORTS BASED ON HUMAN GOALS.

WHY CAN YOU NOT SEE THAT!?

IF ALL YOU HAVE IS CHEAP RETORTS, WHY ARE YOU EVEN HERE?

HMPH... THIS IS WHY I CAN'T STAND HUMANS.

YOU CLAIM THE MORAL HIGH GROUND, YET WHAT BASIS COULD BE GREATER THAN THIS!?

THE TRUE LORDS OF CREATION PLACE ALL SPECIES BEFORE THE PROSPERITY OF ONE!

186

COMPARED TO US YOU ARE NOTHING BUT WORMS...

WE FEED OFF YOU AND PRESERVE THE BALANCE OF ALL SPECIES!

...OR PARASYTES.

BAM

BAM

BAM

SHOOT HIM! FIRE!

GOT
HIM!

WE GOT
THE
BOSS!
WE DID
IT!

SPLAT

HE
WAS...
HUMAN...

WHAT?

CRASH

WHAT?

TAMURA REIKO TOOK A KEEN INTEREST IN HIM, AND HAD ALL SORTS OF PLANS...WHICH END HERE, I SUPPOSE.

NEVER DID UNDERSTAND HIM.

HIRO-KAWA?

!!

I TOOK CARE OF THE OTHERS.

· · · · · · ·

I IMAGINE HE SEEMS VERY STRANGE TO YOU, AS WELL?

YOU LOOK PALE, OFFICER...

F-FROM THE ASSEMBLY HALL?

ド゛ド゛
BAM
BAM
ガ゛ド゛
BAM
ガ゛ガ゛
BAM
゛...

QUITE THE COMMOTION IN THE ASSEMBLY BUILDING...WHY AREN'T THEY REPORTING IN?

ド゛
BAM
ド゛
BAM
゛...

BAM

HEH...

MOST OF THEM WERE HIDING ON THAT SIDE? MY MISTAKE.

AUGH, MY ARMS HURT! KNIVES ARE SO MUCH BETTER.

URAGAMI... YOU...

AWESOME! HIS ARM FLEW OFF!

BAM!

AND WITH THIS SUPER MONSTER CARVING A WAY OUT OF HERE, I CAN FINALLY GET AWAY...

CHAPTER 55: THE END

DON'T ACT SURPRISED, OFFICER! I'VE GOT THE DEATH PENALTY EITHER WAY!

CHAPTER 56: HEAD

!?

PLOP

WE DON'T KNOW THAT. NOT UNTIL WE'RE SURE THEY CAN ELIMINATE GOTO...

SHINICHI, WE SHOULD LEAVE. THERE'S NOTHING ELSE WE CAN DO HERE. WE'RE DONE.

...THIS ISN'T LIKE YOU, MIGI.

THIS IS WELL BEYOND ANYTHING WE CAN INFLUENCE.

FORGET THAT. THE HUMANS ARE WINNING EASILY! IF THEY HAVE TO THEY CAN USE A MISSILE, OR SOME NAPALM.

THE MAIN HALL IS ALMOST FINISHED.

I CAN SMELL IT FROM HERE.

THEY AREN'T SENDING BACK VIDEO.

WHAT'S HAPPENING WITH L.C. YAMAGISHI'S MEN IN THE OTHER BUILDING?

I HOPE URAGAMI'S BEING USEFUL...

HI...EVERY-THING'S GOING SMOOTHLY.

INSPECTOR, IZUMI SHINICHI WANTS TO CHECK THE MONITORS AGAIN...

IT'S NOT THAT...

LOOKS LIKE MEAT SAUCE...

BUT IT ISN'T PRETTY.

TINKLE

SMASH

SMASH

EEK! AUGH!

BAM!

BEHIND US!

WHAT?

ONLY ONE! BUT SO FAST....!

REPORT! HOW MANY?

THE WEIRD ONE HE MENTIONED... THE FIVE-IN-ONE?

ONLY ONE!?

SHOTGUNS AREN'T WORKING!

LET'S GO!

UNH!

BAM

BAM

WHAM

GRAGGHH!

WE'LL AMBUSH IT HERE!

DON'T MOVE!

WHEN YOU SEE THE WHOLE BODY, EVERYONE FIRE!

FIRE!
FIRE!!

BAM BAM BAM

BAM BAM BAM

HOW CAN IT MOVE LIKE THAT!?

AUGH!

WHOOM

SPLAT

I-IN THAT ROOM!

HE'S DODGING BULLETS!?

AUUGHH!

SCRUNCH!

GUH...

D-DON'T SHOOT...

NOT JUST DODGING! ALSO USING SHIELDS.

BAM

BAM

FIRE! THEY'RE DEAD ANYWAY!

BAM BAM BAM

NOTHING LIKE THE OTHERS!

NEVER THOUGHT HE'D BE THIS STRONG...

WE SHOULD FALL BACK!

WE NEED MORE SPACE...

THE ROOF!

AND IN A NARROW HALL LIKE THIS, WE'RE IN DANGER OF SHOOTING EACH OTHER...

BOUNDING OFF THE WALLS AND CEILING...

HURRY!
FALL BACK!

TO THE
ROOF!!

CHACK
チャッ

POOM

COUGH, COUGH

I'VE GOT A BAD FEELING...

EH?

GO!

Y-YOU MEAN, IT ISN'T DEAD?

CAN'T TAKE ANY CHANCES! IF IT WASN'T A DIRECT HIT...WE NEED TO REGROUP ON THE ROOF! HURRY!

THIS ENEMY IN THIS PLACE...
BAD COMBINATION.

AUGH!
IT'S ALIVE!

HURRY!

THOUGHT SO...

PSSSHT!

WALLS AND CEILING ARE THE SAME AS THE FLOOR TO HIM...

WE CAN'T DO A DAMN THING INSIDE!

RIGHT INSIDE THEIR NEST!

WE'RE TRAPPED!

WE HUMANS MADE THIS BUILDING...

BLAM!

CRUNCH!

CLANG!

TO OUR SHAME!!

BUT THEY TURNED IT AGAINST US...

WE CAN FIGHT HIM HERE!

RIGHT, SPREAD OUT!

NO WAY...

...BUT SOMEONE ELSE WILL HAVE TO TAKE CARE OF THE MESS.

YOU'RE ALONE. I TOOK CARE OF THE REST...

THERE ARE GAPS THAT COULD HARM ME.

I'M NOT PROTECTING EVERYTHING.

IS THERE ONE IN YOUR BODY?

HOW ARE YOU DOING THIS?

I SLIPPED UP ONCE OR TWICE TODAY.

TNK

TNK

POP

CLANG CLANG CLANG CLANG

CLANG CLANG

CLANG CLANG

CLANG

CLANG CLANG

BUT AT AN ANGLE LIKE THIS...

CLANG

CLANG

CLANG

CLANG

EVEN IF YOU HARDEN YOUR CELLS, IT'S QUITE DANGEROUS TO TAKE A BULLET HEAD ON.

FOOM

BAM BAM

RRAGH! MOCKING ME!

KA-BOOM!

DODGING BULLETS DOESN'T MEAN I CAN MOVE FASTER THAN THEM.

BUT IF YOU WATCH YOUR ENEMIES EYES AND HANDS, YOU CAN READ THE PATH.

THUNK

!!

WHAM!

GUH!!

. . .

AN EXPLOSION?

ON THE ROOF!

...Y-YOU?

WH-WHAT ARE...

GUH... GRAH...

WHAT ARE YOU?

AN ANIMAL?

ISN'T IT OBVIOUS? A WILD ANIMAL.

...MAYBE I SHOULD HAVE BROUGHT A FLAMETHROWER...

...AN ANIMAL....

...CLEAR!

THAT'S THE LAST OF THEM!

WHAT?

SIGH...

NO RESPONSE FROM L.C. YAMAGISHI!

LOOK OUT!

AH! HEY!!

THEY'RE FINISHED? BUT...

SOME-THING'S FALLING!

TKK

HEY!
HOLD
YOUR
POSI-
TIONS!

WHAT'S
ALL THE
FUSS
ABOUT?

MM?

HEY...

AND YOU WERE HERE...

IT WAS A BIG FIGHT, AND THE OTHER PARASITES ALL DIED...

SO YOU WERE PART OF THIS...

IF I KILLED YOU, I'D FEEL A LITTLE BETTER.

A LITTLE PIECE OF UNFINISHED BUSINESS.

THAT DOESN'T EVEN MAKE SENSE!!

I SHOULD KILL YOU... AND MOVE ON.

BAM BAM BAM

BAM BAM

OH GOD...

ALL AIMED FOR THE HEART. VERY IMPRESSIVE.

AND I'M A LITTLE TIRED.

GET YOU NEXT TIME. SO MANY DISTRACTIONS...

SHOO...

I-IZUMI-KUN! WH-WHAT DID HE WANT WITH YOU?

H-HE FLEW...!?

THIS IS BAD. NEXT TIME WE'LL DIE!!

H-HOW COULD I?

I...I DON'T KNOW!

CHAPTER 56: THE END

TKK

CHAPTER 57: HERO

FIFTY-THREE DEAD... MOSTLY UNDER L.C. YAMAGISHI'S COMMAND— WHICH MEANS *HE* KILLED THEM.

THAT ONE MONSTER COMPLETELY CHANGED THE COURSE OF BATTLE*!*

WAIT!

YOU'RE HIDING SOMETHING ELSE, AREN'T YOU?

DO YOU REALLY NOT KNOW?

THAT COULD HAVE SAVED THOSE MEN?

SOME-THING...

A SEVERED HEAD!

A HEAD!

I'M NOT! I HAD NO IDEA HE WAS THAT STRONG!

A HUMAN HEAD FELL OFF THE ROOF!

235

SHINICHI....

HAHH HAHH
HAHH HAHH
HAHH

WHOOM

SHINICHI...
WHAT A
TERRIBLE
DREAM...

...WHAT?

237

UNFINISHED BUSINESS.

HE'S COMING FOR ME, RIGHT?

I SHOULD KILL YOU...AND MOVE ON.

I CAN FEEL IT.

ANY DAY NOW.

IF WE GET SOME HELP... UDA...?

DON'T GIVE UP SO EASILY.

SO WE'RE DEAD?

NO!! WE CAN'T GET HIM MIXED UP IN THIS.

AND THAT WOULD BE OUR FAULT!

HOW? EVEN IF WE DID, MOST OF THEM WOULD DIE...

THEN HUMANS. GET THE ARMY UP AGAINST HIM AGAIN...

HEH HEH HEH HEH HEH... MIGI...

SO?

DAD... I MIGHT BE LEAVING SOON.

MOM...I MIGHT BE SEEING YOU SOON.

YOU NEVER CHANGE, DO YOU?

239

WHAT SAY WE RUN FOR IT?

HE WOULDN'T CHASE US ALL ACROSS JAPAN, WOULD HE? MIGI?

HA HA HA HA! SCHOOL!

AH! I FORGOT TO GO TO SCHOOL...

TKK

TKK

BOING

・・・・・・・

HAHH HAHH HAHH.

RIGHT, MIGI?

MIGI WOULD NOTICE IF HE WAS CLOSE...

WHAT AM I DOING?

D-DON'T BE NAUGHTY! COME ON!

SLEEPING?

242

IF HE CAME NOW!

HEY!

EEK!

THUMP

S-SORRY!

NOT GONNA APOLOGIZE?

ON YOUR KNEES.

DUDE, WHAT A WUSS!

WHAT A LOSER.

SHEESH.

I'M REALLY, REALLY SORRY.

AHHHH!

KONK

244

WHAM!

THUD

THUNK!

BAM

BUT YOU HAD TO GO AND...

I SAID I WAS SORRY!

I APOLOGIZED, DIDN'T I!?

EEEEK!

...A MESS.

YEAH, I'M REALLY...

YOU BAD BOY.

YOU SKIP TODAY?

WHAT'S WITH YOU?

A TOTAL LOSER.

53 DEAD

STOP!

SHOVE

HEY! LET GO!

HAHH HAHH HAHH.

SH- SHOULD I CALL THE COPS?

DASH

COME BACK! POLICE! POLICE!

IZUMI-KUN....

SIGH...

HEH HEH....
HEH HEH
HEH HEH...

HAHH...

HAHH HAHH.

GETTING AS FAR FROM HERE AS WE CAN? MIGHT BE A GOOD IDEA, SHINICHI.

YOU'RE AWAKE NOW?

OH...

RUNNING AWAY...AND I WAS SO CLOSE TO GRADUATING.

GRADU-ATION TRIP?

PFFT.

SOME-ONE'S COMING.

ARE YOUR SENSES GETTING DULL?

WHAT?

· · · · · · · ·

HEY.

WE SHOULD TALK...

AND MY PARENTS ARE AWAY.

COME WITH ME.

IT'S COLD OUT HERE.

ALL LIVING THINGS SHOW THEIR TRUE COLORS IN DANGER...AND I'M PATHETIC.

THEN SURE...

THERE'S A VOICE IN MY HEAD SCREAMING, "I DON'T WANT TO DIE."

53 DEAD

I WANT TO LIVE....

I WANT TO KEEP ON LIVING...

SATOMI...

I'VE CALLED MIGI COLD-BLOODED HUNDREDS OF TIMES...

MURANO SATOMI DIDN'T ASK ME ANYTHING.

I SURVIVE BY DESTROYING WHAT'S AROUND ME.

BUT I HAVE NO RIGHT TO DO THAT.

YOU'RE VERY COOL.

SHINICHI-KUN...

NO MATTER WHAT!

I WILL SURVIVE...

I HATE TO BREAK THE MOOD, SHINICHI.

WE WON'T MAKE IT HOME. WE NEED TO RUN. NOW!

SERI-OUSLY?

. . . .

TURN THE CORNER!

HE ISN'T MOVING HIS BODY...BUT AT THIS SPEED, HE MUST BE DRIVING.

I CAN PICK HIM OUT NOW. HE'S MUCH STRONGER THAN THE OTHERS! IF WE GO HOME HE'LL EAT YOUR DAD.

IT'S REALLY HIM? YOU'RE SURE OF IT?

YOU CAN'T MEAN...

THIS ONE.

INTO THE PARKING LOT?

BUT WE CAN'T JUST...

YES, WE'RE STEALING IT.

YEAH... OUR LIVES DEPEND ON IT.

EXACTLY!

CLUNK

NO TIME TO WASTE!

CLICK

PUT YOUR SEATBELT ON. I MEAN IT.

I'LL DRIVE.

I DON'T HAVE A LICENSE.

SCREEE

AHH!
HEY!!

I LEARNED
JAPANESE
IN A DAY.

MIGI,
WHEN DID
YOU LEARN
HOW TO...?

VROOOM...

ブオオオ

GIVEN GOTO'S LEGS, HE CAN MOVE FASTER ON FOOT, BUT HE'S YET TO GET OUT OF THE CAR.

BUT AT THIS SPEED, HE'LL CATCH US...

STRANGE FEELING...

OH, YEAH...

WONDER WHY?

EVEN FOR HIM, CATCHING A CAR AND CUTTING US OUT OF IT IS HARD WORK...AND MAYBE HE LEARNED FROM LAST TIME.

WHAT?

MIGI, CAN I ASK A FAVOR?

FIGHTING IN TOWN WILL JUST GET PEOPLE KILLED. THE WALL OF FLESH WON'T WORK WITH HIM.

....

WE SHOULD DO THIS AWAY FROM PEOPLE.

PLEASE.

MIGI...

...FINE. I THOUGHT OF A FEW MOVES THAT'LL WORK BETTER WITHOUT PEOPLE AROUND.

WE'VE COME A LONG WAY... HE'S STILL BEHIND US?

YEP, ALL THE WAY.

HE'LL CATCH US EVENTUALLY, SO WE SHOULD TAKE THE FIRST MOVE.

ALMOST...

NOT THAT ONE...

NO...

MM, THAT SHOULD DO IT.

WHAT'S HE THINKING?

VROOM....

SCREE....

SCREE....

YOU SURE THIS IS A GOOD IDEA?

SHINICHI, TAKE OFF YOUR SEAT BELT.

VRRRRRRRRRR

IF NOT... OH WELL.

IF IT WORKS, WE WIN.

ON TARGET, I THINK...

PARASYTE 7: THE END

"The characters in *Parasyte* are so realistic they all look like people I've seen before. This makes me even more curious what they're going to do next. One of the fake psychics looked just like me!"
(Gunma Prefecture, Dodoria, 19, Student)

"I didn't realize this until I introduced Uragami, but extremely evil characters (or extremely good ones)—and extreme characters—are very hard to draw. Probably because they don't feel realistic. Lots of writers claim you just have to create characters with strong personalities and let them do what they want, but making characters with realistic, strong personalities is another challenge."
(Hitoshi Iwaaki)

(From *Afternoon*, December 1993)

"Is it impossible for humans to acknowledge life-forms other than themselves?"
(Hyoga Prefecture - You-chan)

"It wasn't really a conscious plan on my part to depict mankind as the bad guys, but quite a lot of people find the parasites' actions a lot less horrific than those of the humans. This volume, for example; I was only trying to make everyone act naturally, the soldiers like soldiers, the average citizens like normal people, but it ended up like this. Personally, I don't spend a lot of time deploring my own species..."
(Hitoshi Iwaaki)

(From *Afternoon*, April 1994)

THE READERS ASK, THE AUTHOR ANSWERS

"Goto told Hirokawa he could escape the building easily. What kind of power does he have? I'm looking forward to finding out!"
(Gunma Prefecutre, Nazo wo Toke, 16, Student)

"When Hirokawa ended up dying rather easily, without escaping, some people may have been rather taken aback. But I don't think it's accurate to say Hirokawa was powerless. Given his supreme confidence in his own moral superiority, in a sense he was actually harder to deal with than Uragami. It might be that Hirokawa did not die, but will soon be born..."
(Hitoshi Iwaaki)

(From *Afternoon*, May 1994)

"I think Goto is starting to develop human emotions in a very different fashion from Tamura Reiko."
(Kanagawa Prefecture, Kana Fan, 20)

"Goto's recent actions can hardly be described as unconscious or instinctive. Migi and Tamura Reiko's actions could hardly be described as purely mechanical or practical either. But I think something about them fundamentally prevents them from getting along with humans. I have no idea how many species on Earth are capable of coexisting happily with human beings, but how would humans react to a creature they don't understand, which is not friendly at all? This is one of this story's themes."
(Hitoshi Iwaaki)

(From *Afternoon*, July 1994)

THE READERS ASK, THE AUTHOR ANSWERS

TRANSLATION NOTES

Japanese is a tricky language for most Westerners, and translation is often more an art than a science. For your edification and reading pleasure, here are notes on some of the places where we could have gone in a different direction or where a Japanese cultural reference is used.

Parasytes, page 187

The original rhetorical device has Hirokawa referring to humans as parasites, or *kiseichuu*, and then correcting the last kanji from "insect" to "beast," forming the title of this chapter and the series as a whole. For that reason, I've used the unconventional "y" spelling, even though I've consistently spelled the word with an "i" while referring to the parasites themselves. In Japanese, neither word is used to refer to the monsters. Instead, they're called *parasaito* in katakana. The suggestion here is that the Parasyte in the title is, in fact, humanity. Or at least, that's my take on it. I hope the translation reflects that!

Bad dreams, page 237

The way Migi phrases this in the original Japanese suggests he had the same dream, but English doesn't seem to make that as clear.

Preview of Volume 8

of PARASYTE

We're pleased to present you with a preview from volume 8.
Please check our website (www.delreymanga.com) to
see when this volume will be available in English.
For now you'll have to make do with Japanese!

あっちだ……
胴体を倒さねば

はやく逃げろ
シンイチ!!
こいつはまだ
パワー充分だ!!

でも……いま
すぐそっちへ
……!

くるな!!
2人とも死ぬ
ことはない!!
早く行け!!

だってミギ……

ぐあっ!!

これで……
お別れだ……

さようなら
シンイチ……

シンイチ……

いちばんはじめに
きみに出会って
きみの……
脳を奪わなくて
よかったよ……

おかげで
友だちとして
……いろいろな
……楽しい……
思い出を……

MUSHISHI

YUKI URUSHIBARA

THEY HAVE EXISTED SINCE THE DAWN OF TIME.

Some live in the deep darkness behind your eyelids. Some eat silence. Some thoughtlessly kill. Some simply drive men mad. Shortly after life emerged from the primordial ooze, these deadly creatures, mushi, came into terrifying being. And they still exist and wreak havoc in the world today. Ginko, a young man with a sardonic smile, has the knowledge and skill to save those plagued by mushi . . . perhaps.

WINNER OF THE KODANSHA MANGA OF THE YEAR AWARD!

Now a live-action movie from legendary director Katsuhiro Otomo (*Akira, Steamboy*)!

Special extras in each volume! Read them all!

VISIT WWW.DELREYMANGA.COM TO:
• Read sample pages
• View release date calendars for upcoming volumes
• Sign up for Del Rey's free manga e-newsletter
• Find out the latest about new Del Rey Manga series

RATING   OT AGES 16+

The Otaku's Choice

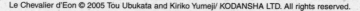

TOMARE!

STOP

YOU'RE GOING THE WRONG WAY!

MANGA IS A COMPLETELY DIFFERENT TYPE OF READING EXPERIENCE.

TO START AT THE *BEGINNING*, GO TO THE *END*!

THAT'S RIGHT!

AUTHENTIC MANGA IS READ THE TRADITIONAL JAPANESE WAY—FROM RIGHT TO LEFT, EXACTLY THE *OPPOSITE* OF HOW AMERICAN BOOKS ARE READ. IT'S EASY TO FOLLOW: JUST GO TO THE OTHER END OF THE BOOK, AND READ EACH PAGE—AND EACH PANEL—FROM RIGHT SIDE TO LEFT SIDE, STARTING AT THE TOP RIGHT. NOW YOU'RE EXPERIENCING MANGA AS IT WAS MEANT TO BE.